The Gospel According to Elihu

The Gospel According to Elihu

Moses Pollard

BookLocker
Trenton, Georgia

Print ISBN: 978-1-958877-09-8
Ebook ISBN: 979-8-88531-292-9

Published by Booklocker.com, Inc.

Printed on acid-free paper.

2022

Library of Congress Cataloguing in Publication Data
Pollard, Moses
The Gospel According to Elihu by Moses Pollard
Library of Congress Control Number: 2022919112

Table of Contents

Introduction

Much has been written about the pain and agony that Job had encountered in his life. Many sermons have been preached about the patience of Job, and how his latter days were better than his former days. It is well noted that, through no fault of his own, Job was singled out by God to be considered for Satan's temptation, and ultimate humiliation.

Many people have asked the question: Why? If Job was a perfect and upright man, as the Bible depicts, then why was he dealt such a cruel hand? Why would a loving God allow a fallen, disgraced, and disgruntled angel (Satan) to attack the one man who was unlike any other man in the land of Uz?

Why does God get such a bad rap from believers and non-believers when tragedy comes into someone's life? Is God the problem? Why did Job have to suffer? Where does the story of Job leave us? Are we even worthy of "consideration" to be tested? These and other similar questions arise in the minds of people who believe that God is the one to be blamed for their troubles, and the troubles of others.

This book will explore many of these hard questions in an attempt to give the reader a view of God's perspective according to His word. I will not profess to have all the answers to all the mysteries surrounding the life of Job, or in the word of God, but some answers are simply displayed in written form by inspired men of God on the pages of the Holy Bible.

Some questions may only be fully explained at the time of our true revelation of Jesus Christ and when we see Him face to face.

The purpose of this book is to discuss the importance of what the young orator and friend of Job, Elihu, had to say about the sovereignty and nature of God. Elihu's message, though it was written in the days of the Old Testament, is very timely and relevant to Christians today. His message surpasses time because it illustrates how God speaks to, and through, mankind to provide the correct information and knowledge to the right person, at the right time in their lives. Elihu's humbled but timely message speaks of the good news of God's grace and mercy. It is God's grace and mercy that separates Christianity from any other religion because grace and mercy cannot be obtained through man's futile attempt to justify himself through works. Elihu, though younger and less influential than Job's other friends, awaits his turn to address the misleading advice and spiritual ignorance being spoken to Job by the others.

Elihu identifies that the main cause of problems in our lives is not God, but rather man's inability to spiritually comprehend the spiritual nature of God. The "good news or gospel" is revealed to us from Elihu's perspective throughout this book. I pray that each reader of this book will allow the Holy Spirit to individually speak to their personal hearts as the spirit reveals himself in truth, according to the will of God.

Chapter One
Stop Blaming God for Your Troubles

Have you ever been guilty of blaming God for troubles in your life, or problems in the lives of your loved ones? I have heard people who wrongfully make negative comments about God bringing about calamity in someone's life. One example is statements we hear in the media, such as, "This is an act of god." This points a finger at God as the perpetrator of an evil event. Yet, seldom do we go to the biblical word of God to determine just where these attacks originated. Do they originate from the bosom of a loving God who loved mankind so much that he offered up His own begotten son as a ransom for the sins of one man?

To blame God for destruction, mayhem, and disorder in the lives of the very souls that he sent His son to save is like the New Testament religious leader's assertion that Jesus himself was a devil who was casting out devils.

God has a plan for each one of us and, yet, he has given us the autonomy to choose the path by which we should travel. God also, according to

His written word, empowers man to speak to situations, storms, and mountains and, with the tiniest of faith, still the storm, and move the mountain. So, we must withdraw from blaming God for troubles in our lives because He has already given us power and authority over it.

"The Gospel According to Elihu" is a for real, in your face look at how we personally but unjustly complain about God's role in our lives when we are the ones in control. Elihu's message will serve as a reminder to all of us about the importance of trusting and relying of God in all matters, and in all ways, according to His word. The message is simple yet profound in that God loves humanity, and desires for all of mankind to be in fellowship with him. This book will serve as an announcement of just who God is and the fact that He does not need any of us to tell Him how to be God. Simply said, God cannot be explained in the words of men. He must be revealed in men's hearts.

This book will use Job's plight as an example to show the reader a more spiritual approach to life's challenges. Without revealing the entire plot of this writing, we will show the reader that they, not God or their circumstances, control their outcome.

It is time for the body of Christ to come clean, and admit that we don't always like the way things happen to us, as well as our family, while we are in the process of serving God. We put on a good face in public but, deep down inside, some of us do question God's timing, absenteeism, and seemingly inability to intervene in a tragic situation. If we could be honest with ourselves, there are times when we have the attitude of Martha, the sister of Lazarus. She said, "Lord, if you had been here, my brother would not have died.

"Martha's attitude was one of disappointment in the un-timeliness of Jesus because He showed up several days later than He was expected. If you really notice in this story, both sisters, Mary and Martha, had an attitude toward Jesus because the Bible says that Mary did not even come out of the house to greet Jesus. It appears to me, from my many years of ministry, that there are still some Mary and Martha attitudes toward God. When a loved one died, or we received a bad medical report, an eviction notice, experienced a divorce, or endured other life-changing events, were we expecting a specific intervention by God? And, if so, why did it not happen? The first thought that comes to mind is "Lord, if you had been here, my brother would not have died." The question is: Was God to blame for your troubles? Was God at fault when death occurred when His word says that it is appointed once for man to die? Did not His word declare that not even death can separate us from His love? Is it not in His word that He went to prepare a place for us and, if He has prepared that place, that, one day, He will come to take us to the prepared place?

Let us remember that God's perfect plan for our lives will often differ from the imperfect plan that we want to paint for ourselves. In our plan for our lives, we draw out a design that is based on our limited scope of knowledge. We generally are not able to comprehend the vast complexities of life changing circumstances that may lie just around the bend in the road. In David's famous 23 Psalm, he writes that God leads him beside the still waters. If God is doing the leading, we will surely obtain the promised goal for our lives but, if we are doing the leading, we could end up in places where we should not be. This does not mean that being led by God is going to be an easy, unobstructed road to your Godly life's goal. But, the outcome will still result in you reaching that goal in God's perfect timing. David was led by God but, if you have read and paid attention to the life of David, during the course of his journey, there were many pitfalls, stumbles, and detours. But, he did accomplish the goal that God had set for his life.

One of David's setbacks in his pursuit of his promised kingdom occurred as he attempted to be a leader and fighter for God's cause. David's role as troop leader almost ended in tragedy. While David and his exiled troops were out fighting a battle, their families were taken captivity by the Amalekites, from the camp at Ziklag.

What a stressful situation it must have been to return from battle only to see smoke rising up from the direction of your camp in the distance! When David and his men arrived in the camp, there was nothing and no one there. In their grief and despair, David's soldiers considered stoning him to death because they thought they had lost all that they had in lives.

David went before the Lord, and inquired as to what he should do. Shall I pursue after the men who attacked our camp, asked David of the Lord.

Pursue, answered the Lord. Following God's direction, David and his men pursued the men, and retrieved all that they had lost. Not one woman or child had fallen to any harm.

In this story, David could have reacted like many of us would, by placing the blame for our problems on God. We may have considered our mission a failure because it did not go as smoothly as we wanted it to go. We could have quit, given up, retreated, or just simply stopped believing. Yet, David did what anyone who believes that God should do the leading in their lives should do, and that is to enquire of the Lord as to what direction we should take. Those of us who depend on a GPS (Global Positioning System) to navigate from place to place understand that, when we come to a detour, he GPS will re-direct our travel. The same goes for our lives when we are being led by God. The enemy may place a detour in your path but God will direct you around, through, over, and under the obstacle that's blocking your progress.

In David's Ziklag experience, we notice that he did not blame God but, rather, he encouraged himself in the Lord. What we can learn from this story is how David's wisdom to go before the Lord with his dilemma is the exact same way that we, as believers, should conduct ourselves. David and his men all grieved until they had no more tears to shed. But, unlike his men, David went to the Lord for answers. David's men discussed the prospect of stoning him to death because their losses. But, killing David would not have returned their loved ones to them. David's men represent the inability of men to place their trust in God but, rather, to trust in their own understanding. If these men had followed through on their threats, and had killed David, they would have doomed their loved ones to slavery or death. The resolution to your dilemma lies in the hands of God but you must trust him to be your deliverer.

God is not the author of confusion in the lives of believers, He is our savior. God is the author and finisher of our faith and the just shall live by faith. As I have stated before, God has a plan for each one of us. The key is to allow Him to lead and guide us throughout His plan. Rejoice in the knowledge that God has all things in control. I used to read a comic strip in the local Sunday newspaper called "Family Circus."In this comic strip, there was a post of the mother sending a son out to the mailbox to retrieve the mail. The son, who appears to be six to eight years old, goes out the front door of the house to the mailbox, which is not more than 30 feet from the front door. But, instead of retrieving the mail, and returning it right away to his mom, he takes an adventure throughout his neighborhood. In the comedic depiction by the artist, dots are used to illustrate the path that the son took as he went to visit some of his friends, to the park, past the local store, through the backyard, and other activities which had nothing to with retrieving the mail from the mailbox. Our lives sometimes are like "Family Circus" in the way we venture off course from where God wants us to be. And, when things did not work out for us, we blamed God.

David said, "He leads me in the path of righteousness for His name's sake." The key to that verse is that God was leading David. It does not depict that David was leading himself. We must always allow God to do the leading because we are the sheep of His pasture and sheep are to be led. Sheep depend on a shepherd to lead, and guide, and care for them. When we take David's advice about being led, we have no reason to blame God for our troubles because God never leads us astray.

Chapter Two
Dominion

The book of Genesis states: "In the beginning, God created the heavens and the earth; and the earth was without form and void." The fourth and fifth words of the book of Genesis say "God created," which means a supreme being created the heavens and earth. The Hebrew name for God in this context is Elohim, or the plural name for God.

The beginning of all existence as written in the Holy Bible was the work of a perfect God. This creation, as described in the Holy Scriptures, was to have occurred over a period of six days, and brought about a day of rest for God on the seventh day. On the sixth day prior to resting on the seventh day, God created a special creature called man. This genesis of everything in God's Kingdom lays the ground work of a beautiful one-on-one relationship between God and the mankind that He created.

The focus of this chapter is to tie in the significance of the sixth day of the creation of man to the importance of God's grace and mercy throughout the Holy Bible. The book of Genesis is like a contractor, laying a good foundation of a great house, who knows that the key to a stable house is a great foundation. Likewise, God used the book of Genesis to dig into the Earth below the frost line, and pour the concrete footings of the foundation of understanding of the extreme love that He would have for all of humanity.

Therefore, in the Genesis of God's creation, He establishes the beginning of His relationship with man, and set in place a perfect foundation in Christ, even before man allowed himself to be tricked out of his grace-filled relationship with God. In Genesis, we are introduced to man and his intimate relationship with God, which is thwarted by the enemy's trickery. The story of the first man, Adam, depicts a fall from grace to the point of seemingly falling completely out of the grace of God.

God never gave up on mankind and, to the contrary, placed a lifeline for all of humanity throughout time in the form of Jesus.

In the narrative of Luke 6:46-49, Jesus describes characteristics of a good disciple. The type of man who Jesus speaks of in these few verses is one of very strong resolve and wisdom. Jesus, the earthly son of a carpenter, uses the analogy of building construction as an illustration of how one must build a strong foundation. In this writing, Jesus describes for us the proper way to build a strong spiritual relationship with him. Jesus' vivid analogy of the storm in this story makes it clear to each of His listeners that proper footings is what supports the stability of any substantial structure.

In verse 48, Jesus says that the flood waters arose, and beat vehemently upon the house. Notice that Jesus did not reference an average storm or casual waters, which may be withstood by a house, built on inferior footings. Rather, Jesus describes a violent, destructive, atmospheric storm with treacherous winds beating against a man made structure. The word of God from this writing of the Bible refers to very tumultuous, violent waves pushed by hurricane force winds. Jesus wanted the reader to clearly understand that he was describing a life-threatening situation. A house in a storm of this magnitude requires a very strong foundation to resist the constant barrage of pounding waves.

To put this story in the correct prospective, we must understand that Jesus is the savior of the world who came to redeem falling man. Savior is the English translation of the Greek word sótér, which means a savior, deliverer, or preserver. One author used the analogy that the word "Soter" is like a person who is standing on the edge of a high, dangerous cliff, about to fall to their death, but is suddenly snatched back to safety by a deliverer. Thus, so was fallen man because of the sin of Adam and Eve in the Garden of Eden.

The world needed a savior to redeem mankind, who was spiraling out of control. They would have been forever lost to sin from their birth. God, in his infinite wisdom, sent his only begotten Son to be the propitiation for fallen mankind. Why did God do this? John 3:16 reads: "For God so loved the world that he gave his one and only Son, that whoever believes in him shall not perish but have eternal life."God sent his only begotten son because he loves us. God loves us regardless if we are rich or poor, black or white, and heterosexual or homosexual. I know to some eyebrows will be raised when I say that God loves a homosexual but it is true. In that famous salvation verse of scripture, notice that it reads that God so loved the world. It does not mean that

God loved the Earth but, rather, every human creature who resides on the Earth. The term "world" describes mankind, regardless of their state of salvation. It designates God's love toward all who are born into a sinful world based on the sin of Adam, and the fall of mankind from the Garden of Eden. Therefore, with the love that God had for every human, he wanted none of them to perish; to live in eternity in damnation. Rather, his desire was that all would surrender their lives to Jesus Christ, and spend eternity with Him in glory.

God intended for mankind to have dominion over the Earth, and everything in it. God placed man in a perfect place where he could live in peace and harmony throughout his life. The Garden of Eden is described as a place where man was in total control over his own destiny. In the Garden of Eden, man was like a god over the animals, plants, and sea creatures. The whole garden belonged to, or was under the control of, Adam and Eve. Adam had the authority to name everything in the garden the way he wanted to name it.

In the garden, there was no sin until Adam disobeyed God's command, and broke a kingdom principle of trust. By breaking the trust in his relationship with God, Adam relinquished his authority and, in turn, gave it over to Satan.

In the Kingdom of God, our relationship with Him is based on our trust in Him. God trusts us to obey his commandments. We must trust God in all our ways, and not depend on our own understanding.

The Holy Bible says that the kingdom of God is not meat or drink, but righteousness, joy, and peace in the Holy Spirit. The kingdom of God is not those things that we most closely associate with as being life's necessities. We consider meat and drink as a physical daily necessity to survive. Scripture tells us that God's word is to be considered more precious or important than our daily bread. This means that our physical needs are never to be placed above our spiritual relationship with God.

To understand the kingdom of God, we must first have a clear understanding of how God operates.

To understand how God operates requires us to immerse ourselves in His written word, as described in the book of Joshua, and in Psalm

One. In these two writings, the focus is on meditating in the word of God, both day and night.

Then, says the scriptures, the one who follows these steps will have success.

Further, we must gain an understanding of the foundation of His word from a spiritual perspective. God is a spirit and they that worship Him must worship Him in spirit and in truth (John 4:24, KJV). God cannot be truly understood from a physical perspective only, but of the spirit. Understanding spiritual matters does not come naturally for the believer. We are taught from a very young age to trust in our physical feelings for survival. We are taught that, if we smell smoke, we should be aware that there is a fire. If we feel heat coming from something on the stove, don't touch it. But, it is not the same when comprehending spiritual matters. This is certainly true in the life of Jesus. Some scriptures clearly reveal that the disciples who walked, talked, and communicated with Jesus daily were often confused by his teachings, as related to spiritual aspects of the divine nature of God.

Jesus understood the level of understanding of his disciples. Therefore, He taught them by using terms that they could understand, such as agricultural and fishery terminologies, to explain the things of the spirit of God.

This level of teaching was necessary to show the gospel to persons from a perspective of their understanding. Agriculture and fishing were two of the most important economical means of survival during this time. So, the local people could relate to terms concerning their livelihood.

Jesus used the simplest elementary school teachings regarding the five senses to show His disciples, as well as His audience, the nature of God.

The senses of touch, sight, hearing, feeling, and taste were all used in many of Jesus' teachings to contrast or explain the Kingdom of heaven. In one instance, Jesus explained the difficulty of a rich man inheriting the Kingdom of Heaven as he compared it to the impossibility of a Camel passing through an eye of a needle.

In this analogy, anyone could visualize a huge camel trying to enter through an eye of a needle and, thus, surmise that a person depending on riches alone would find it impossible to inherit the Kingdom of Heaven.

It is interesting to note that the footing of a house is seldom viewed by the owner of the house. Yet, if that important work is not properly constructed, the entire structure will tumble to the ground, or sink deep into the Earth.

In the kingdom of God, it is the unseen realm that becomes of far more importance, in the outcome of our lives, than those things which are seen. For the things which are seen are temporal. Visible things are temporary. These temporary things do not have eternal or everlasting value.

While we look not at the things which are seen, but at the things which are not seen: for the things which are seen are temporal; but the things which are not seen are eternal.

II Corinthians4:18 (KJV)

In the Kingdom of God, it is the unseen realm that becomes of far more importance in the outcome of our lives than those things which are seen. Nothing that we see on this earth will follow us into Heaven.

We can use financial debt as an example of an earthly issue, which can cause us great agony in our daily lives. Financial debt is a temporary earthly issue; however things of the spirit are forever.

Anyone of us could accumulate a tremendous amount of debt in our lifetime. While the debt is looming over us, as like an eclipse of the sun, we feel like there is no escape insight. Yet, when we overcome the debt, by either paying it off, filing for bankruptcy, or having it dissolved by some other legal means, it is no longer an issue to us at all. Why? It was not a permanent situation. It was temporary. In the highlighted scripture above, the Apostle Paul tells the Church at Corinth to look beyond the temporal or visible things because, as a disciple of Christ, we should look toward spiritual things. There is a real world of things not seen by the naked eye, which are in the supernatural. They are eternal. While we do not see them with our natural senses, they are more real than the things that we do see naturally.

There was a story of a college professor who was an Atheist who tried to do everything within his power to disprove the existence of God. One day, standing before his class, he explained that God did not exist because no one had seen Him.

This professor, like many non-believers, underestimated the power of true spiritual thinking coming from the mind of a man or woman of God. As the professor pontificated before his students about the non-validity of God, he noticed that one of his students had raised his hand high in the air, and would not take it down until the professor acknowledged him.

The student was a freshman from a small Christian community in the mid-west of the United States. The professor peered anxiously at the student, waiting to hear what was to be said to defend the existence of God. As the humble, spirited student slowly rose from his seat, and began to refute the professor, the entire student body sat motionless, waiting to see what would transpire.

The student said, “Professor, is it your theory that God does not exist because we cannot see Him?”

The Professor replied, “That is correct.”

The student began walking to the electrical outlet on the classroom wall, “Well, come over here, and stick your finger into this socket, and prove to us that electricity does not exist."

While that may be a funny story, it illustrates the point that things do exist even if we cannot see them. It also illustrates the point that, even if we cannot see a thing, it can still affect our lives.

But the natural man does not receive the things of the Spirit of God, for they are foolishness to him; nor can he know them, because they are spiritually discerned.

I Corinthians 2:18 (KJV)

Two decades ago, I was attempting to hang a ceiling fan in the ceiling of the master bedroom of my home. To mount the support bracket, and complete the wiring, I had to go up into my attic. I cautiously turned off the circuit breaker that I thought powered the light in the ceiling of the room I was working in. I even double checked to be sure that the ceiling light was not burning, thus proving that the electrical power to that light was no longer engaged. I then mounted the bracket, and fed the wiring through the bracket opening. As I was feeding the wires through the bracket, two of the wires touched each other and, suddenly, I was struck with 110 volts of electricity.

The jolt was so great that I was ejected by the force onto the floor. Dazed and confused, I tried desperately to visualize what had just happened. I did not see the electricity with my natural eyes but boy did I feel it! Now, if you ask me if electricity is real, although I cannot see it, or smell it, or taste it, I can answer to the affirmative that it is very much real.

The spirit or supernatural realm in which God operates is real, but is not visible to the natural eye. The supernatural exists as plainly to God and those who operate in the supernatural, or with spiritual discernment, as the natural world exists to a natural man.

An excellent illustration of the supernatural realm and its relevance as it coincides with our natural world is found in the writings of the Old Testament.

In Second Kings 6:15-17, as the prophet Elisha was surrounded by the host of the Syrians, his servant saw them, and franticly pointed out this discovery to the man of God. Elisha's first response to his servant was to say to him, "Fear not." To show the servant that God is all powerful and that, even when we cannot see His mighty works, they are still present, Elisha asked God to open the servant's eyes so he could see into the supernatural.

Now, the servant's natural eyes were fine for a natural vision but, to observe the things of God in the invisible realm, he needed a supernatural vision. To peek into the supernatural realm requires an opening of our natural eyes. Throughout the Bible, God uses visions, dreams, and actual live occurrences to show us that the supernatural realm is just as real, even more real, than the natural realm that we are accustomed to. In some of these communications of the supernatural realm, God provided wisdom, knowledge, guidance, encouragement, understanding, and insight into some future event. The servant's understanding of the wisdom of Elisha could not be comprehended without God's intervention and revelation.

By unveiling the hidden secret that only God's prophet could see from a supernatural perspective, he gave the servant a wealth of knowledge in just a few seconds.

The servant could see very well. Most likely, the servant had 20/20 vision in the natural. We cannot see the things of God with our natural eyes. Thus, we must use spiritual discernment.

God is a spirit and they that worship Him must worship Him in spirit and in truth.

John 4:24 (KJV)

Notice this verse of scripture says that God is a spirit, in other words a supernatural spirit.

Paul, in his letter to the Corinthian Church, said the things that have been taught to us by the Holy Spirit are taught comparing spiritual things with spiritual things. We must never attempt to understand spiritual matters with a carnal mind. Why? Because, things presented from a spiritual perspective are just foolishness to a carnal minded person. Jesus was asked by His disciples why He taught in parables. His reply was that it was not meant for those carnal minded listeners to comprehend the things of the glory of God. Jesus knew that they were not in a spiritual thinking mindset to receive the super natural things he was teaching.

When God opened the spiritual eyes of Elisha's servant, he saw with supernatural vision for the first time. What he saw with supernatural eyes was legions of angels on chariots of fire surrounding the army of the Assyrians, ready to do battle with them. Now, the angelic beings were there all the time but the servant could not see them. It is only when we are seeing through the supernatural that these things are revealed to us.

The Assyrian's army did not physically see the army of angels on chariots of fire. The army was totally unaware of the vast number of angelic hosts, yet the angels were present. Elisha and his servant saw them because they were allowed by God to see into the supernatural realm.

Be not forgetful to entertain strangers: for thereby some have entertained angels unawares.

Hebrews 13:2 (KJV)

Some of us have been in the company of angelic hosts unaware because we did not use our spiritual discernment. The spirit realm surrounds us and, yet, most of us are oblivious to its existence because we are attempting to see the world through natural eyes.

The point is that, as we lay the foundation of spiritual growth before you, it must be received by your spiritual mind.

"Your understanding of the things of God can only be broadened if you allow your mind to reach beyond what is visible to your natural eyes."

(M.P)

This is obviously a significant statement in the story of Job because Job is certainly oblivious to the conversation between God and Satan, which takes place in the supernatural realm.

Job could not see or hear the conversation, nor was Job even aware of the spiritual significance of the conversation. Job's level of understanding was limited to the information and knowledge available to him in his natural realm. It does not mean that the supernatural realm did not exist during Job's days on earth. It simply means that Job could not comprehend it.

Did Job believe in a supernatural God? Yes, of course he did because Job religiously made sacrifices to God. The godly relevance with which

God placed on Job's dedication to serving Him proves that God trusted in Job's love for Him.

Therefore, it is important for us in this time of history to have a more vivid understanding of God than Job had in his days on Earth. The way for us to obtain a clear understanding of the very nature of God is to first seek to understand the supernatural realm of God.

When God developed the Earth, He spoke all things into existence. In the first chapter of the book of Genesis the writer lays the intricate footings which will be the very foundation of all existence of the Earth, animals, and mankind.

The Bible describes how God, in the beginning, laid out all the natural and supernatural necessities for mankind to use to exist on Earth. Notice that, in all of His creation, God used supernatural means to do it.

God then passed that ability on to man to speak things into existence, the same as He did.

When God placed male and female on the plot of land that the Bible refers to as the Garden of Eden, He provided provisions to exist comfortably throughout their lives was there.

Notice that, in Genesis 1:26, God spoke into existence the power of dominion into the lives of man and woman. God said, “Let us make man in our image, after our likeness: and let them have dominion. Dominion is an absolute power. It was to be over everything on earth, which includes the earth's atmosphere. Dominion was given by God to mankind to control and rule over all things on earth.

We must understand that, once God gave mankind that dominion, He never took it from them. This verse tells us that we have dominion over everything. Everything in this earth is under the power and authority of man. This dominion was given to mankind over all the earth.

And God said, Let us make man in our image, after our likeness: and let them have dominion over the fish of the sea, and over the fowl of the air, and over the cattle, and over all the earth, and over every creeping thing that creepeth upon the earth.

Genesis 1:26 (KJV)

I am sounding redundant because I want you to seriously look closely at the word dominion as it pertains to mankind, and the absolute power that it holds.

The word dominion is the same word used as reign, master, or rule over the earth. The Hebrew word for dominion is "memshalah." It means to have authority, domain; to rule or to govern over something or someone.

There is no doubt that God intended for man to rule over the earth. When you evaluate the substance of the earth today, it is easy to understand that all of it was prepared for man to exist on throughout the time that God has placed him here.

The earth houses rich deposits of herbs and minerals that have existed in the earth from the beginning of time. These same herbs and minerals are being discovered daily, and then used for healing and life-sustaining purposes, as they were intended in the beginning. Some are now used in medicines, to counter the ill effect of diseases, which did not exist during the time that man was placed in the garden. Sickness resulted from man's disobedience to God and, thus, his fall from grace. In many instances, the medicines that are marketed today are simply a chemically-derived substitute of a natural cure placed in the earth by God, from the existence of the earth. This is certainly demonstrated by the action of Moses when he was instructed by God to place a tree into the bitter waters in the wilderness of Marah.

Notice that Exodus 15:20-26 details the fact that undrinkable bitter water was turned to sweet, drinkable water by the use of a tree, which was already in existence before the arrival of the Israelites. Certain herbs and spices are known to have the ability to cure particular aliments. These herbs existed from the formation of the earth and more have yet to be discovered. Inventor and author George Washington Carver discovered many uses of a peanut through what is described in his memoirs as knowledge gained through meditation with God. So, just think about how many more hidden truths lie in the undiscovered uses of trees, plants, minerals, and herbs already on and in the earth.

God gave man dominion over it all earthly things yet we have not fully accepted the full power of that dominion.

To utilize our God given dominion, we must first train up our minds to think like God, and for our mouths to speak like God, and our faith to be in God.

"To utilize our God given dominion over the earth, we must train our minds, mouth, and thoughts to be like God."

(M.P.)

Training is super important to God because He understands that mankind is born into a sinful realm. No one has to teach a little, innocent child how to lie, it comes naturally. You could walk into a room with only the child present, see a broken glass on the floor, and ask, "Who broke this glass?" And, you will receive the reply, "I don't know."

Wait, you don't know? You are the only one in the room. Lying is a natural thing to do, as a form of self preservation. Now, where does it come from? Sin entered this world through the sins of Adam and Eve and mankind has been sinning ever since. What we have to know is that we have to overcome what is natural by training our minds with the mind of Christ.

First, we must be born again into the knowledge of Jesus, the Christ. This occurs by the regeneration into a believer by doing what the Apostle Paul describes in Romans 10:9, which is believing in your heart and confessing with your mouth that Jesus is the son of God and that he died for our sins, has been resurrected, and is in Heaven, seated on the right of the Father. Once this regeneration occurs, we are new creatures but we still have some megabytes of stored up, old thoughts, actions, and patterns of the past that have to be trained out of our minds.

Our tempers may not be restored to a new patient temperament without first training our minds to think like Jesus. Our patterns in life may not automatically convert to be Christ like just because we have been converted. If a new convert religiously left work daily, and went to Joe's bar and grill for dinner and drinks, then that new convert must train his mind to avoid going to Joe's bar and grill. These earthly patterns become a way of life and they are often separating us from coming to the full knowledge of Christ. The aunt who always leaves church go home, and then call her sister to gossip about what went on in church, will continue this pattern of behavior until she trains her mind to do otherwise. It is simply why we often can't stay on a restrictive food diet. Once the mind and body is accustomed to eating and drinking certain foods and beverages, they will always crave those things that may not be good for you.

Training one's mind is not a simple feat because it involves the same type of process that it took to get to that same point from the beginning.

"The training of our mind to the things of Christ is a process, which begins with great faith."

(M.P.)

As it is with most habits in life, they resulted because of a process. We did the same things that we did, day after day, in the same manner and those things became a way of life. So, for us to change that pattern of life we must change the process and we change the process by changing our mindset.

Distant runners have to train their minds along with their body. For the runner, he must make it resistant to pain, distractions, and environmental issues to effectively endure the grueling conditions of a distant run. The mind will tell the runner that the pain in his side is a sign of a sickness but the trained mind will push past that. The environment may appear to be unbearably harsh in the runner's mind but the person trying to train it for harsh running conditions will say, "I must make my body press on."

As a believer, we must make our mind know the word of God as it reveals His will for our lives, and to subdue our minds to come into full compliance with God's will. It is as simple, in some cases, to train yourself to begin each day with a positive Bible-based confession of faith. When we religiously do that, day after day after day, then it becomes second nature to us. Every time you open your eyes, the first thought should be to say a positive confession over your life. Before the smell of the aroma of coffee from the coffee pot can penetrate the smell sensors of your nose, you will automatically think "positive confession." It becomes learned behavior. It becomes a way of life.

A great example of training up our mind is found in the story about the conversion of poet and clergyman John Newton. Newton was involved in slave trading, and was at sea during a tumultuous storm. His ship was being battered by the wind and waves. Knowing he would likely not survive caused him to call on help from a God who he had no previous relationship with. The writer of the legendary song "Amazing Grace" depicts the vast change of heart from a lost sinner to one saved by grace. Newton's conversion did not immediately cause him to end his slave trading activities but it certainly was the beginning of the inevitability of the end of his ungodly activity. We have to train our minds to think, talk, and walk in a manner pleasing to God. It is the examples that Jesus' set forth, as a human being, that helps us to understand how to treat people in various aspects of our daily lives. It takes a trained mind to do that. To know to evaluate circumstances before we react in situations. To think godly before we think earthly. Although these things sound simple, just picture the many times in our daily lives where we could have assumed the role of any unbeliever in certain situations. When the clerk at the store gives you incorrect change, or when the auto repair shop adds a repair item to your bill that was not discussed in his estimate. Do we react in a godly or ungodly manner? Is it because we are so filled with the Holy Spirit or is it because we have trained our hearts to always speak in love. Our human hearts need to be trained because Jesus said, O generation of vipers, how can ye, being evil, speak good things? For out of the abundance of the heart the mouth speaks. A good-hearted man will generally speak good things, but an evil-hearted man will speak evil things. Which mind do we have in us?

Often, believers have allowed Satan to confuse and diminish our God granted dominion to fit with his agenda. However, dominion over the earth was granted to mankind, stolen by Satan using trickery and deceit, but returned to man by the sacrifices of Jesus, the Christ.

God not only gave man dominion but he also taught Adam how to use this authority. In Genesis 2:19-20, God made the animals, and brought them to Adam to see what Adam would call them. Look at dominion in progress. Whatever Adam called the animals became their name. This process of allowing Adam to speak into existence names of fowl and animals expressed the dominion, or rule, that God had given him over them. The pleasure of having dominion was necessary for man to live among animals without fear or intimidation.

Adam even named the type of person that God had given him, by calling her "woman," one made from his body.

In Old Testament times, a servant could not go boldly to the throne or even in the presence of the king. The person who did that would be instantly killed. The book of Esther illustrates the danger of entering in the presence of a ruling king without permission.

As heirs of salvation, we must develop worship with God where we are compelled to boldly enter in His presence. Hebrews 4:16, states that we are to go boldly to the throne of God. This passage of scripture differs from the perspective from which I was taught as a young Christian. As a young believer in Christ, we were taught to humbly approach the throne of grace. This would seemingly be the way that God would have his servants come into his presence. If we were to sit at a dinner table with our earthly father, we should feel comfortable in his presence to ask of him things that he has available to provide to us. That is unless we have a very awkward and dysfunctional relationship with him.

Jesus said in Matthew 6, or what man is there of you, whom if his son ask bread, will he give him a stone?

Job made sacrifices to God and he worshiped God from the limited knowledge of worship that he was capable of understanding. Job did not have a son-ship relationship with God. Job did not fully understand the importance of true worship with God.

True worship begins with an understanding of who God is in relation to who you are to Him. Explaining this may seem convoluted in a very narrow understanding of scripture but, in simple terms, even the least knowledgeable believer can comprehend the premise.

What is mankind that you are mindful of them, human beings that you care for them? 5. You have made them a little lower than the angels and crowned them with glory and honor. 6. You made them rulers over the works of your hands; you put everything under their feet: Psalm 8:4-6 (NIV)

Is man not the heir of salvation and are we not going to be in charge in over angels, when we reign with Christ?

As we look at the latent fingerprint of what occurred in the book of Job, we will gain a clearer understanding of the true nature of God. We will also gain a stronger sense of who we really are in God's kingdom. Like Job, our later days will far exceed our former days when we illuminate our minds to where we walk by faith, and not by sight.

I pray that this book will open your spiritual eyes to understand that God is love, not the cause of our problems in this life. God esteems mankind in high regard. So much so, that He delivered to us the greatest gift of all eternity in the form of His son, Jesus.

Chapter Three
The Parasite in Paradise

This chapter is a prerequisite to understanding the reasons why mankind has suffered through many centuries under the duress of a parasitic attack by the enemy, and the importance of a savior as an antidote to that attack.

God's plan for mankind was very simple. Man was to obey Him, and share a wonderful relationship together with God in paradise.

Man was simply charged with the tending to of a land that was given to him, with power to speak things into being. Dominion was given to man if only he would not transgress God's law as it pertained to two trees in the garden.

In his loving way, God allowed man the autonomy to make his own decisions, which, in one sense, shows how much God loves us and, yet, on the other hand, God seems to give mankind more credit for following instructions than we deserve.

To clearly understand what really occurred in the Garden of Eden; let us define the word parasite. Below you will find an online website dictionary definition of the word parasite. It does not clearly define the way the enemy, which is Satan, deals with people, but you will grasp the concept of taking something that is not yours.

Notice, in the definition, it says that a parasite derives nutrients from its host at the host's or victim's expense. The parasite was not invited but it attached itself, or snuck in, by some type of trickery or deceit.

Dictionary.com; defines parasite as: an organism that lives on or in an organism of another species, known as the host, from the body of which it obtains nutriment.

The Holy Bible clearly defines Satan as a deceiver of the whole world. Satan is also described as a liar, and the father of all lies. Several passages present Satan as this crafty being who fell from grace and who is now on the rampage against mankind to destroy it. Let us examine this parasitic being who intends to destroy all of us by trickery and deceit.

Look at what is written in the book of Revelations about Satan.

7. And there was war in heaven: Michael and his angels fought against the dragon; and the dragon fought and his angels, 8.And prevailed not; neither was their place found any more in heaven.9.And the great dragon was cast out, that old serpent, called the Devil, and Satan, which deceiveth the whole world: he was cast out into the earth, and his angels were cast out with him.

Revelation 12:7-9 (KJV).

Here, John describes an event where there was a war in the heavens. Satan and his angelic allies fought against the Arc angel Michael and Satan's conspirators lost. Thus, Satan and his angelic followers were cast out of heaven to the earth.

Isaiah describes Satan as one who aggressively sought to be equal or greater than God, and was cast down to hell to the sides of the pit. Isaiah says that those who see him will look narrowly upon him and say:

Those who see you stare at you, they ponder your fate: "Is this the man who shook the

earth and made kingdoms tremble, 17 the man who made the world a wilderness, who overthrew its cities and would not let his captives go home?"

Isaiah 14:15-16 (NIV)

Satan has attempted to cause havoc everywhere he has been. He is the one who latches on to people as if he was a parasite and nibble away at them until they are destroyed or he is cast out.

One of the most interesting stories in the Bible is about David being tempted by Satan to number the children of Israel. Notice in the above verse how crafty Satan is by inciting David to number Israel. By stirring up a little pride in David, Satan caused great wrath to be brought upon God's people.

I Chronicles 21:1, *God was very displeased with the census, and he punished Israel for it.*

Satan knew from his own dilemma that God despises a prideful spirit so the deceiver used that knowledge to cause David to commit a great sin. David's actions caused 70,000 men of Israel to be killed.

Eden was described in the Holy Bible as being a paradise, a perfect place, where man did not have to wont for anything. I could imagine it to look like one of the lush green sections of land in Hawaii, with beautiful waterfalls, palm trees, rivers of water, and beautiful flowers. I imagine that the pools of water that sprang off from the four rivers that ran through it were crystal clear and that the grass was as soft and plush as that on a professionally manicured golf course green. Eden was perfect in every way except for one thing. There was a parasite living in the area. This parasite devised a scheme to destroy this special paradise, as well as the man and woman who God left in charge of it.

Satan is a parasite who invades into places where he has no business at all, like in the lives and minds of those who are blood born believers in Jesus, the Christ, and their children, and in the affairs of believers who have committed their life to serving Jesus.

The good news is that, even with all his schemes and devices, Satan is still a defeated foe, existing on borrowed time because the word of God says that he loses in the end.

Verses 10 and 11 in Revelations 12 let us know that we are the victors in this eternal race.

And I heard a loud voice saying in heaven, Now is come salvation, and strength, and the kingdom of our God, and the power of his Christ: for the accuser of our brethren is cast down, which accused them before our God day and night. 11. And they overcame him by the blood of the Lamb, and by the word of their testimony; and they loved not their lives unto the death.

Revelations 12:10-11 (KJV)

"They triumphed over him by the blood of the Lamb and by the word of their testimony. There is no power in Heaven or earth greater than Jesus. It is his blood that was shed for all the earth that makes the difference for all eternity. *They triumphed over him by the blood of the Lamb and by the word of their testimony,* is a victory chant for all believers. It is not in our strength or might. Nor is it our blood that is shed to accomplish this feat. It is the blood of Jesus the Lamb slain before the foundations of the world. It was the sacrifice of Jesus on the cross on Golgotha's hill that destroyed the yoke of bondage that Satan had placed on all of humanity, both dead and alive, as a causative effect of Adam's sin in the garden.

The blood will eventually destroy the parasite so that, during the millennium reign of Christ, the Devil will be bound while people will live in true paradise.

Chapter Four
Understanding Grace

Freedom for the saints of God begins when we learn to understand the value of the gift of grace.

Being justified freely by his grace through the redemption that is in Christ Jesus.

Romans 3:24 (KJV)

Grace is often misunderstood as it relates to the body of Christ. Yet it is grace that is the most important blessing given to us from God. Grace is described in the Bible as God's unmerited favor. Grace is a gift of God. None of us can earn or obtain it by humanistic natural resources, nor by an inheritance. Man's fall from grace was a supernatural occurrence. Therefore, to regain grace requires a supernatural, spiritual intervention to make it available to us. From the writings of the New Testament we find that the Apostle Paul described grace to the believers in Rome as a redemptive blessing through Christ.

The New Testament writing of the book of James 4:6, But He gives more grace. Wherefore He saith, God resisteth the proud, but giveth grace unto the humble.

This gives us the understanding that grace is not to be taken lightly, but it is a gift of God to those who will humbly recognize that we cannot of ourselves give ourselves this supernatural gift

James describes the recipient of this gift of grace as one who is willing to recognize the power and authority of God. In doing this one act of humbleness before God, we receive more grace.

8. For by grace are ye saved through faith; and not of yourself (it is) the gift of God. 9. Not of works, lest any man should boast.

Ephesians 2:8-9 (KJV)

When I was a young Christian boy growing up in Gloucester County, Virginia, the only thing that I knew about grace was that it was a prayer spoken before dinner.

The church that I was baptized in did not teach us about grace. Especially, not as it pertained to the true definition of the word according to scripture. It may have been due to the number of sermons that focused more on hell and damnation than on grace and God's love for mankind.

We were taught that, if you sin, you would go to hell. The Church did not explain the difference between un-confessed sin and living in sin. It was confusing how God could be so cruel, to send us to hell if we committed one sin, even if we were sinless in every other aspect of our lives. It was not explained to me that many of the characters of the Bible, who we trusted and believed represented God, were men who sometimes failed in their faith walk. In fact, the Bible openly exposes the fallacies of men and women of God. Yet, God is a forgiving God.

Let us look at Peter, one of Jesus' disciples. Peter said to Jesus that he would die for Him before he would allow anything to happen to Jesus. Jesus rebuked Peter, and said, "Before the rooster crows, you will deny me three times."Peter went on to do exactly what Jesus had said yet Jesus forgave him of his sins. In the 17th chapter of the book of Acts, the writer says that, in times past, God winked at the ignorance of man but now he calls all men to repent.

If that previous verse was not about God's grace, then I am at a loss as to a better definition.

"If we confess our sins, he is faithful (Jesus) and just and will forgive us our sins and purify us from all unrighteousness."

John 1:9

Notice in this scripture that the author uses the plural (sins), meaning more than one, and the plural (all) unrighteousness.

The only one with the power and authority to grant such a request is Jesus, the Christ. The scripture reads, "He (Jesus) is faithful and just."

Only Jesus is faithful, meaning that he totally accomplished all that God sent him to complete here on earth. Jesus was faithful to God to the very end of his mission. Jesus is just because God made him our advocate. I want to raise an expectation for the reader of this book to fully enjoy the gift of grace in our everyday lives. Understanding grace will open your eyes as a result of his faithfulness in carrying out his assigned mission. Jesus said, "I came to do the will of my Father who sent me." Because Jesus accomplished His mission without committing a sin, He was justified to die for our sins.

Grace can be defined as God's unmerited favor but I want to explore deeper into the depths of this cave of misunderstood blessings.

To fully understand grace, we must first understand the spiritual nature of God. God is a supernatural being. In the book of Numbers, God is described as not being a human who has the capability to lie. Instead, if God promises, then those promises must come to pass.

God is not human, that he should lie, not a human being, that he should change his mind. Does he speak and then not act? Does he promise and not fulfill?

Numbers 23:19 (NIV)

Man has the capability of lying because of being born in sin but God is a spirit, and was not born in sin. Mankind is not able to always fulfill our promises. Thus, a statement unfulfilled becomes a lie. If God speaks it, it must come to pass. God said, "Let there be light," and it was.

Since grace is God's unmerited favor then, once God grants it to us, no one can take it away. Once God promises a thing to us in his word, nothing can stop us from receiving it. In the story of

Balaam, in the book of Numbers, chapter 23, we find a clear picture of the power of God's word. A king named Balak tried to bribe a prophet of God, Balaam, to curse Israel. But, the prophet said, "I cannot curse what God has blessed." There is no power that that can curse God's blessings. Balaam simply explained the law of God as it relates to a blessing or a curse.

16 And the Lord met Balaam, and put a word in
his mouth, and said, Go again unto Balak, and
say thus.
17 And when he came to him, behold, he stood
by his burnt offering, and the princes of Moab
with him. And Balak said unto him, what hath
the Lord spoken?
18 And he took up his parable, and said, Rise
up, Balak, and hear; hearken unto me, thou son
of Zippor: 19 God is not a man, that he should
lie; neither the son of man, that he should
repent: hath he said, and shall he not do it? Or
hath he spoken, and shall he not make it good?
20 Behold, I have received commandment to
bless: and he hath blessed; and I cannot reverse
it.

Numbers 23:16-20 (KJV)

So, the grace of God surpasses all understanding, it transcends beyond barriers both man made and supernaturally devised. When His grace abide in our lives no one can we are assured that are truly blessed.

Chapter Five
In the Land of Uz

Some theologians have said that the land of Uz was likely located between the city of Damascus and the Euphrates River, and to the southeast area of Edom. This is based somewhat on the home place of one of Job's friends, Eliphaz. Eliphaz was from Teman, which was a well-known city in Edom. Records of historical scholars have concluded that the land of Uz was a real place during biblical days.

It is not important as to where the incident involving Job occurred. What is important is that Uz could be anywhere. The land of Uz is only relevant because Job resided there. What about where you live? Is it relevant because you live there?

In every part of this world, we experience the same types of encounters that Job had to deal with. Wars and rumors of wars existed even during the days of Jesus. Earthquakes happened then, and are happening now.

Let us look at the land of Uz from a Biblical perspective. How is it important to us? How does the land of Uz compare to where you are today?

It all begins in the Garden of Eden. The second chapter of Genesis begins its narrative by explaining that God made provision for man before man was ever placed there.

Genesis 2:8 And the Lord God planted a garden eastward in Eden; and there he put the man whom he had formed.

One of the wonders of God is that He always knows what we have needed even before we know that we needed it. The Endemic man had no point of reference to judge whether being in the garden was a good thing. All this man knew was that he was in a place of beauty.

Later, in the first two chapters of Genesis, two major events occur. God makes the first covenant with man, known as the Edenic Covenant. In Genesis 1:28, the covenant declares that Adam would replenish the earth with children, use nature for his physical needs (food and shelter), have dominion over the animals, to eat fruits and vegetables, to labor for his sustenance, and to obey God's rule of not eating from two trees (forbidden fruit) in the Garden. These six covenant rules were to be obeyed by Adam.

The second event was that the caring infinite God saw that Adam was the only creation without a mate. Therefore, God made a woman (Eve) for him, a helpmate.

Now man had all the resources available to him that he would ever need to sustain his life. Adam had a beautiful place for him to dwell in all the days of his life. Man was all set for a paradise of happiness.

Job lived in a land called Uz and there was a sense of paradise for him and his family. God had caused Job to prosper in the land of Uz. Job's wellbeing from a financial perspective was seen by the locals as a true blessing.

In Job's town, he was considered to be a man of impeccable character. He was blameless in all respects, and living an upright life before the Lord. Job was reverent of God's supreme power. He put away any thoughts or acts of evil.

In the land of Uz, Job had a wife, seven sons, and three daughters. The sons and daughters lived in their own dwellings in the area of Uz. Job was very concerned about the salvation of his sons and daughters. Therefore, he regularly made sacrifices of animals before God for them.

Job owned seven thousand sheep, three thousand camels, five hundred yoke of oxen, five hundred female donkeys, and a very great household. Job was the richest man in the land of Uz.

For all practical purposes, the land of Uz was a blessed place for Job and his family. The life of Job let us know that we can live in a blessed place, and still endure hardships. We may also be living in God's grace, and still endure hardships.

The area where we live, in and of itself, does not eliminate hardships or strife unless, like Job, there is a hedge of God's protection around you. A rich person, who is able to amass a great fortune of wealth, may still die of an incurable disease even if he lives in what many consider a blessed place.

The land of Uz represents just how wealthy the saints of God can truly be and that there is nothing spiritually wrong with being wealthy. Job never allowed his possessions to be gods in his life because he openly expressed his commitment to his God. We must become accustomed to living in the spirit, and not in the materialistic wealth of this world. We certainly can be blessed to possess many things in this world but the land of Uz should not be our eternal dwelling place. The Bible says that, when we depart this place, there is a building not made with hands, eternal to the heavens. The land of Uz cannot be compared to what awaits us in Heaven. The number of livestock or houses, and the amount of wealth over in the land of Uz is just a glimmer of the goodness that God has prepared for those who love Him. Imagine living forever in a place where the streets are paved with gold. Where there is never any darkness and where the glory of God lights the heavens. Job truly understood that the land of Uz was not his final dwelling place.

Chapter Six
It Just Does Not Make Sense

As Jobs' friends continued to assail him with a barrage of accusations, name blaming, and finger pointing, this once wise man began to make unrealistic statements in defense of God. The problem arose out of ignorance of God's omnipotence and because of Job's limited earthly understanding of the true spiritual nature of God. Job's earthly view of the traumatic events that had consumed him to this point in his life clouded his mind, leading to obscurity of what is really happening in the supernatural. We must understand that, at the time of Job's dilemma, there was not a complete Old and New Testament Bible available for him to read and study, nor to obtain God's word for healing. Through the years there have been many great Evangelist preaching faith for healing on television, and providing written guides for divine healing in bookstores all over the country. In fact, the end of the word of God that says "we win" was not even written yet. There was no written word from the book of James that said, "***Is any sick among you? Let him call for the elders of the***

church; and let them pray over him, anointing him with oil in the name of the Lord: 15 And the prayer of faith shall save the sick, and the Lord shall raise him up; and if he have committed sins, they shall be forgiven him.

James 5:14-15 (KJV)

All that Job had to rely on was his trust in God from the first five books of the word of God (The Pentateuch, the scrolls, and Psalms), and a belief that he had lived a holy life in the presence of God. We criticize Job for his lack of faith but he did not have as much information as we have. Yet, with all of the information available to us today, we still struggle with faith issues.

In the book of Job, he was been cast into a role that he had not studied for, and was sorely unprepared to accept. If only Job had the advantage of knowing what the Apostle Paul wrote to the Church at Ephesus: "*We wrestle not against flesh and blood, but against principalities, powers, rulers of darkness of this world and every high thing that exalts itself against the knowledge of God.*"

The words of Apostle Paul let the believer of today know that the battles we are facing are not to be contended with against flesh and blood, or in opposition to a human being. Rather, these are battles instituted by supernatural powers, and supernatural beings, with the sole intent to destroy the saints of God. In that sixth chapter of the New Testament book of Ephesians, the Apostle Paul says to battle these spiritual attacks with spiritual armor. Paul's descriptions of the pieces of armor are designed to protect the saint in every vulnerable area of their existence, similar to the equipment of protection worn by Roman soldiers of that day. The Roman soldier's armor was designed to protect all vital areas of their bodies, including their feet. Likewise, in spiritual battles, we must protect our vital areas, and also carry a weapon of warfare.

It is unfortunate for Job that he was unable to see this attack against him, with the full knowledge of who, the attacker was, and the methodology being used. If he had known, he would have prepared himself. If we knew what tomorrow would bring, we would be better prepared for what would happen. The ability to fully see into everyone's future is only capable by the Trinity.

God is omniscience. Therefore, he knows the beginning from the end. If Job knew that God had orchestrated this entire chain of events to prove to Satan that there are some saints who will never denounce God, then he would understand why the bleakest earthly situation has no control over God. Job's test may seem cruel to a casual observer because they do not understand the commitment required of God for those who declare their faith in Him. They who truly trust God will believe in Him through any and every adversity in life.

I remember a story from elementary school that best illustrates the behind-the-scenes discussion and interactions between God and Satan about Job. Remember that it was God who inserted Job's name into the equation as Satan explained his escapades of walking to and fro in the earth. Satan stated that he was walking throughout the earth, implying that he had been going about seeking souls to destroy. It was God who said, "Have you considered my servant Job?" Satan immediately took the bait, and said, "Yes, I considered him, but you have a hedge of protection around him and I cannot get to him." Satan obliviously had at least attempted to devour Job and his household but, when he saw the massive security that God had placed around

Job's home, Satan decided to bypass him, and seek others less protected.

In the elementary school story, the sun and the wind were having a contest to see which of the two was more powerful. The wind boasted about how it was so powerful it could blow down large obstacles. The sun bragged about its power also. Finally, the two forces of nature decide to have a contest to see which one was the most powerful.

The sun was very clever so he said to the wind, "Do you see that man walking down the road?

The wind said, "Yes."

The sun said, "Let's see which one of us can make him remove his coat."

The wind took the bait, and hurriedly built up a great puff of cold air, and began to blow upon the man with such force that the man forcibly tugged at his coat to ward off the violent chilly wind. The harder that the wind blew the stronger the man would cling to his coat. Finally, giving up on any hope of making the man take off his coat, the wind said, "Okay, sun, you give it a try."

The wise sun made himself closer, brighter, and hotter than ever before and, soon, the man started to take off his coat due to the extreme heat coming from the sun.

The wind was astonished at how easily the sun had won the battle of power and might but, from the very beginning, it was a staged contest, set up by the sun, which involved the unsuspecting man in the story. Naturally, a hot sun would cause a man to remove his coat quicker than a gushing, frigid wind. But, all the man in the story knew was that one minute he was cold and the next he was very hot.

We seldom know the entire story of what motivates us to go east or west, nor of all of the factors that affect our future.

Just as the sun was much wiser than the wind in that unrealistic elementary school story, so is God much wiser than any of His creation. God knew the motives behind, and standard operation of, the tricks of Satan. The problem for Job is that he didn't know nor could he comprehend the supernatural war occurring behind the scenes.

Job attempted to defend what he perceived was God's wrath, brought to bear upon him for some unknown or un-confessed sin in his life.

Job's assessment of his troubles appears to be in line with a humanistic point of view, but without spiritual knowledge. While we must admire the dedication to a god who Job feels is the orchestrator of his demise, it doesn't make sense. Why? Because God was not the perpetrator of the attack on Job, it was Satan.

15 Though he slay me, yet will I trust in him: but I will maintain mine own ways before him.

Job 13:15 (KJV)

First, let us examine Job's statement. "Though he slay me, yet will I trust him:" I don't know about Job, but I am not thrilled to serve a God who will just slay me for no reason? Job's, philosophy seems to state as its basis that God would himself kill his own children without cause. Job's reasoning makes the application that, even though God would treat him unjustly, by destroying him and his family that he should still serve him.

It just does not make sense. "Though he slay me, yet will I trust him:" Nonbelievers would be quick to point out the inconsistency in serving a God who is not merciful and just? These unsubstantiated random statements about God have caused some people not to trust God. God gets the blame for many things that Satan is behind.

God is a righteous God. The statements cannot be true unless it lines up with God's word. God is a just God. A just God will not destroy the just unjustly. In the book of Genesis, God is preparing to destroy a city of unjust people, but takes the time to justify his actions to Abraham. In the dialog between God and Abraham, it is apparent that God considers all circumstances before he uses mass destruction as punishment.

32 And he said, Oh let not the LORD be angry, and I will speak yet but this once: Peradventure ten shall be found there. And he said, I will not destroy it for ten's sake.

Genesis 18:32 (KJV)

In those verses of scripture of the eighteenth chapter of Genesis, Abraham's pleaded to God, and God's patience during the process, are an example of the merciful nature of God. Although God was justified in destroying those wicked cities, he is also a God of grace and mercy. Abraham's plea was not the deciding factor in God's decision about the fate of those cities because God already knew that there were not ten just men living in Sodom and Gomorrah.

Abraham's lengthy conversation with God about the dilemma facing Sodom and Gomorrah may seem to be meaningless to the casual observer. But, the significance of the spiritual meaning is incredibly important. The relationship of God toward man has been misunderstood and misrepresented for many years, even from the beginning with Adam and Eve.

Abraham gives us a realistic view of a passionate God, rich with love and grace. Only a loving God who loves mankind beyond man's imagination would have the understanding to bear with Abraham's unmerited request for a stay of execution on Sodom and Gomorrah.

The conversation between Abraham and God mimics somewhat the content of a conversation between an earthly father and an inquisitive son. The earthly father perhaps would have allowed his lack of patience to reveal his inability to allow his son continue questioning an already made-up mind. Yet, God continued to allow Abraham to express his humble desire to save a city over the salvation of a few. This story symbolizes the spirit of a God, who loves mankind so much that he is willing to bear with our inadequate desire to question the works of his hands. Abraham lacked the immense wisdom that God possesses. Therefore, he was speaking without all the knowledge necessary to comprehend God's logic. Often we will ignorantly question God without merit and, sometimes, foolishly blame him for our troubles without cause.

When we view God with natural eyes, and not through spiritual eyes, we may mistakenly accuse God of things that the enemy has done, and fooled us into believing that God did it.

Job viewed his dilemma from a natural perspective rather than from a spiritual perspective. Job's statement even appears to be a steadfast, unmovable declaration of his faith in his God. But, it just does not make sense. Why? Because, how can you trust a God who will destroy you?

In the nineteenth chapter of the book of Job, he continues to accuse God of all kinds of atrocities against himself. In that chapter, Job unjustly accuses God of being the perpetrator of his troubles. Verses 5-21 describe Job's pleas to his friends to be merciful toward him. Yet, ironically he does not believe that God could be merciful to him.

5 If indeed you would exalt yourselves above me
and use my humiliation against me, 6 then know
that God has wronged mean drawn his
net around me.
7 "Though I cry, 'Violence!' I get no response;
though I call for help, there is no justice.
8 He has blocked my way so I cannot pass; he
has shrouded my paths in darkness. He has
stripped me of my honor and removed the
crown from my head.
10 He tears me down on every side till I am
gone; he uproots my hope like a tree.
11 His anger burns against me; he counts me
among his enemies.
12 His troops advance in force; they build a siege
ramp against me and encamp around my tent.

13 "He has alienated my family from me; my
acquaintances are completely estranged from
me.
14 My relatives have gone away; my closest
friends have forgotten me.
15 My guests and my female servants count me
a foreigner; they look on me as on a stranger.
16 I summon my servant, but he does not
answer, though I beg him with my own mouth.
17 My breath is offensive to my wife; I am
loathsome to my own family.
18 Even the little boys scorn me; when I appear,
they ridicule me.
All my intimate friends detest me; those I love
have turned against me.
20 I am nothing but skin and bones; I have
escaped only by the skin of my teeth.
21 "Have pity on me, my friends; have pity, for
the hand of God has struck me.

Job 19:5-21 (KJV)

The pitiful state of affairs in Job's view of his declining life is a self-proclaimed assessment of a riches, to rags story. At one point in his life, Job was a wealthy, happily married father of ten, and a well-respected community leader. In a series of disasters, issues, and death, his life appeared to only be hanging by a single thread, with marginal hope in a positive outcome. All of the things that made Job a great man, including his impeccable relationship with God, are all but a fading memory. The state of Job's present life is a perfect example of why we should not blame God for our troubles. First of all, God did not cause Job's problems. Satan did. And, Satan did that in the Garden of Eden when he introduced sin into the world.

In the conversation with God, Satan had already declared that Job was on his hit list of those he wanted to devour. But, the only reason that he couldn't was because God was protecting him and his family. So, Satan was already scheming for a way to get to Job and his family to destroy them. God only pointed out to Satan that some people would not turn their backs on Him simple because they had lost their family, earthly possessions, and "things." Also, we must note that, in every situation, God gives us an avenue of escape or release. We were granted the power of dominion over everything on earth. We were given the position of royal priesthood, and being a chosen generation. We have no right to blame

God for our troubles when God declared that he would never leave us, nor forsake us. The mistake we make sometimes is to blame God without knowing the entire story.

In verse six, Job states, "Then know that God has wronged me and drawn his net around me." Job didn't know the entire story. Job's narrow-minded view of life centered on family, and how God blessed him and his family. A relationship built on one deed rewarding another is a misguided one. "I will worship you, Lord, if you bless me," indicates that, in order for God to have my total heart, there must be some reward for me. Jesus rebuked Thomas after His resurrection because Thomas had stated to the other disciples that he would only believe that Jesus rose from the dead if he was able to see the nail prints in Jesus hands, and to thrust his hand into Jesus' wounded side. Jesus, however, rebuked Thomas, saying, "But blessed are those who believe without seeing."

Blind faith is the only way that we can truly say we have placed our trust in Jesus, without ever seeing Him.

Job reaches a point where he feels betrayed by his family, friends, and God, and cries out for pity from his friends. Job makes a statement that even the children find him repulsive. Pity, in this instance, would be Job's version of justice for this stage of his life. In desperation and despair, Job seems to cling to a wow is me attitude hopelessly feeling as if the entire world as he knows it has come tumbling down on top of him.

Job finds himself absorbed in self pity to a point where one must be concerned about the stability of his mind. Yet, the only glimmer of hope is that he does still possess an inner desire to serve God. He does not truly understand the nature of God, and all of the attributes God possesses, nor does he fully comprehend the compassion of God. His statements are recklessly void of relevance, and without an ounce of merit, but they do represent a sample of a broken human soul searching for the answers to life's pitfalls. It is the loneliest of feelings for a believer to feel like God has turned His back on you, and refuses to answer your prayers, or respond in any way to your cry for help. These were the feelings of Job in verse seven. All of Job's statements are false but his calamity of life causes him believe that they are true. Reality can be clouded by the mysteries of the world, of supernatural occurrences taking place in and around our lives. The key is to develop enough faith to believe the invisible reliability of the word of God in action to perform the will of God in your life.

Chapter Seven
The Gospel According to Elihu

There is much more to be said on God's behalf when it relates to the people of this earth, and their relationship with God. The English word "gospel" can be defined as "good news." Good news is always a welcoming message to our ears, especially during times when we are dealing with series of bad news.

As cold waters to a thirsty soul, so is good news from a far country.

Proverbs 25:25 (KJV)

The "good news" for all of mankind is that God orchestrated the beginning and the end of the age without consulting with anyone on earth. The "good news" is that God is a spirit who has infinite power and control over things seen and unseen. The "good news" is that, with all the omniscient, omnipresent and omnipotent power which God processes, He still gives man a distinct place in His kingdom.

The young character in the book of Job, Elihu, who appears along with Job's three other friends, illustrates an example of an Old Testament Apologetic preacher who steadfastly defends the faith, despite an age inequality as compared to Job's more senior audience.

And Elihu continued, and said, "Bear with me a little and I will show you, for I have yet something to say on God's behalf.

Job 36:2 (NIV)

Elihu takes the approach of a godly man, wise beyond his years, yet very respectful of Job's senior friends, who spoke their thoughts, and then stopped speaking at all. Elihu, waited until what he felt was an appropriate time, and then proceeded to lay out an entirely different analogy of the nature of God than that reported by the older men. Elihu speaks with the authority of a God fearing man, and not as a misguided conformist like his counterparts.

Elihu respectively remains silent throughout the long dissertations leveled against Job by these religious three friends. But, what he spoke was truth and wisdom on God's behalf. As the three men wailed their unfounded comments of their view of Job's failed relationship with God, Elihu patiently waited for the right moment to tell them about the "good news," of the goodness of God.

Elihu simply makes the statement, "Bear with me a little longer and I will show you that there is more to be said in God's behalf." He asked humbly for time to refute their views on the true nature of God, and God's true relationship with mankind. First, Elihu justifies his knowledge by explaining from whom he received his source. Elihu argues that he receives his spiritual insight from a far off source, which is perfect, and that could only be God.

In the fifth verse of the thirty-sixth chapter of Job, Elihu makes the following statement: *"God is mighty, but despises no one; he is mighty, and firm in his purpose."* The Omnipotent power of God is revealed but God's nature of not despising anyone comes to the forefront as he defines aspects of God that were overlooked up to that point.

Elihu explains that, although God is supreme, he despises no one, and is firm in His purpose toward mankind. The scriptures reiterate the statement made by Elihu, saying that God is love; therefore God is not a God who despises His creation. The word of God also states, “For God so loved the world that he gave His only begotten son, that whosoever believes in him should not perish, but have everlasting life.”

Notice in that verse of scripture it reads, that God so loved the “world,” meaning even those who despise Him. It means that God is not petty like mankind. He does not hold grudges, nor does He operate under the shadows of prejudice. It is difficult to believe that God, who makes such a declaration about His character, would then contradict His own statements by despising His creation. Elihu’s views of a righteous God refuted the efforts of Job’s other friends, who shared their sinister views of God as an evil being getting even with anyone who does not live a one hundred percent holy life every day.

It serves notice on us today, as an example of how Christian believers must be ready, willing, and able to give an account of the word of God at any given time, and under any given circumstances, regardless of the status of the person’s prominence or position.

The Prophet Nathan received a word from God to deliver a word of rebuke to King David over

David's infidelity with Bath-Sheba, the wife of Uriah the Hittite. Jesus rebuked many religious leaders of his day over the inadequate interpretation of the law. Paul confronted Peter to his face over compelling non-Jews to be circumcised. It was Martin Luther's 95 Thesis that led to a reformation.

This generation will also have to contend with inadequacies of interpretation of the word of God by those who attempt to manipulate it for their own personal reasons.

In the thirty-second chapter of the book of Job, Elihu finally sees an opportunity to speak on behalf of the Almighty. It is only after the other older and self-proclaimed righteous men ceased to speak that Elihu seized an opportunity to articulate Job's dilemma from a different perspective.

Elihu said:

6I am young in years and you are old; that is why I was fearful, not daring to tell you what I know.

7 I thought, 'Age should speak; advanced years should teach wisdom.'

8 But it is the spirit in a person, the breath of the Almighty that gives them understanding.

9 It is not only the old who are wise, not only the aged who understand what is right.

The Gospel (good news) according to Elihu begins to unfold before the reader, in the chapters that follow, in ways that can only be understood by listening to the spirit of God.

First, Elihu explains to his audience why he was silent while they rambled on in their limited knowledge of how God operates. It is important to understanding the origin of the anger and disgust that Elihu felt toward Job and his friends for unjustly blaming God for their troubles. Elihu said:

6I am the same as you in God's sight; I too am a piece of clay.

7 No fear of me should alarm you, nor should my hand be heavy on you.

8 But you have said in my hearing, I heard the very words.

9 I am pure, I have done no wrong; I am clean and free from sin.

10 Yet God has found fault with me; he considers me his enemy.

11 He fastens my feet in shackles; he keeps close watch on all my paths.

We must pay attention to what Elihu is saying to Job because he is speaking the truth from God's perspective. Elihu says that God does speak but we may be too busy, too noisy, too fearful, or too doubtful to hear him. But, God speaks just the same. Not only does God speak to us and we do not hear him, but Elihu states in verse eleven that God also watches over us in ways that we cannot comprehend.

The good news according to Elihu is that God never leaves us nor does he forsake us. Elihu explains to Job, and all who will listen to him that, when we are asleep, God shows us visions of the future.

Elihu slowly begins to lay out the building blocks of what faith should look like in the eyes of a believer. The faithful believer should have confidence that even though there are no visible signs of God working on the right hand or on the left hand, that he is, in fact, working on our behalf.

Elihu directs these men to the fact that God is not mortal as a man is because God has power to be omnipresent. Elihu says that God keeps watch over all his paths to keep him from hurt, harm, or danger. If Job knew the command given to Satan to touch him, but without authority to kill him, then he would understand Elihu's argument from the beginning. Elihu continues telling his contemporaries that God takes great effort to preserve his saints; to keep them from stumbling.

In the next several verses, Elihu points out that God has already lined up his angelic beings to position themselves to be of service, and to take care of his people.

19 Or someone may be chastened on a bed of pain with constant distress in their bones,

20So that their body finds food repulsive and their soul loathes the choicest meal.

21Their flesh wastes away to nothing, and their bones, once hidden, now stick out.

22They draw near to the pit and their life to the messengers of death.

23Yet if there is an angel at their side, a messenger, one out of a thousand, sent to tell them how to be upright,

24And he is gracious to that person and says to God, "Spare them from going down to the pit; I have found a ransom for them"—'

Only Elihu appears to be wise enough to understand that God was not being unjust toward Job. On the contrary, God was watching over and protecting Job throughout the entire ordeal. Job's other friends leveled their focus on his dilemma based sorely from a humanistic viewpoint without merit.

The Bible says that God watches over his word to perform it. While watching over his word, God is offering security to those who the word is designated for. Not only does God watch over his word but he also offers an additional level of protection to those he loves. God declares, in his word, that he has appointed angels to watch over the elect of his kingdom. Why would God go through all the trouble of appointing angels to watch over his saints, and then turn around, and kill them himself? Jacob spoke about his vision in which he saw a ladder reaching from the floor of the earth to the landing in heaven, and saw the angels of God ascending and descending. These angels were traveling back and forth from heaven to earth, carrying out their mission for God. Another name for angel is "messenger." So, God is constantly communicating with His people.

The previous verses also set the tone for the Gospel of Jesus Christ in that Elihu points out that, even though our lives may be headed toward a pit, God has a ransom for our souls. The good news is that the ransom is Jesus, the Christ.

The Gospel according to Elihu attempts to change the distorted view, which portrays God as an angry god on the rampage against those he has sworn to uphold. To view God's relationship toward his people, with any characteristics other than that of merciful, long suffering full of grace and slow to anger, is an unjust assessment of Him.

Elihu says: ***26"then that person can pray to God and find favor with him, they will see God's***

face and shout for joy; he will restore them to full well-being."

There is great encouragement in the words of Elihu to Job and all who will listen to him. "In verse 26, Elihu describes how a person can receive favor from God through prayer. Elihu goes on to say that, in addition to receiving favor, God will restore them to full well-being. Elihu's description of God's grace and mercy reminds me of the story in the New Testament when Jesus healed the ten lepers. Nine of the lepers went on their way, hoping to gain admittance, and good standing back in their communities, by gaining the approval of the Chief Priest. The nine walked away satisfied with being healed, but still crippled with the deformities to their bodies caused by the effects of Leprosy. Yet, one of the lepers realizing that he was healed, returned to Jesus, and began worshipping and thanking Him for his healing. Jesus asked him, "But, where are the nine?" Then, one leper received the blessing of grace by also being made whole; total restoration of all that he had suffered as a result of Leprosy. Instead of being like the nine lepers, Jesus showed more grace upon the one who returned to give thanks.

In verse 27, Elihu goes on to say; *27* ***And they will go to others and say, 'I have sinned, I have perverted what is right, but I did not get what I deserved.'***

What Elihu describes in verse 27 is, in its purest form, the perfect definition of grace. In scripture, grace is described as God's unearned favor.

3 Praise be to the God and Father of our Lord Jesus Christ, who has blessed us in the heavenly realms with every spiritual blessing in Christ. 4 For he chose us in him before the creation of the world to be holy and blameless in his sight. In love.

Ephesians 1:3-4 (NIV)

You could not earn, buy, or deserve your way into grace because it is a gift of God.

28 God has delivered me from going down to the pit, and I shall live to enjoy the light of life.'29
God does all these things to a person twice, even three times—

30 to turn them back from the pit that the light of life may shine on them.

If the world is ever going to understand the nature of God, it must receive the good news about God's amazing grace. Elihu points out to Job and the other men how God behaves when a person stumbles more than once. Elihu says that God restores them several times over. The good news is that Elihu, to this point has thoroughly refuted the former false claims of God's unjust treatment of Job by his friends.

4 Let us discern for ourselves what is right; let us learn together what is good.5 Job says, 'I am innocent, but God denies me justice.

6 Although I am right, I am considered a liar; although I am guiltless, His arrow inflicts an incurable wound.7 Is there anyone like Job, who drinks scorn like water?8 He keeps company with evildoers; he associates with the wicked.9 For he says, 'There is no profiting trying to please God.'

12 But I tell you, in this you are not right, for God is greater than any mortal.13 Why do you complain to him, that he responds to no one's words?14 For God does speak—now one way, now another though no one perceives it.15 in a

dream, in a vision of the night, when deep sleep falls on people as they slumber in their beds,[16]He may speak in their ears and terrify them with warnings,[17]To turn them from wrongdoing and keep them from pride,[18]To preserve them from the pit, their lives from perishing by the sword.

The Gospel According to Elihu is very simple. Verse 10 says that it is far from God to do evil and God does not do wrong. The things we see and hear that are sometimes confused with an "act of God" are evil things generated by Satan.

Stop blaming God for your troubles. God is not the author of confusion and He is not the cause of havoc and despair in the lives of His saints. In the words recorded of Jesus speaking to His disciples, we find that Jesus clearly defines who the perpetrator of evil is in our lives. In John 10:10, Jesus says, ***"The thief comes only to steal and kill and destroy; I have come that they may have life, and have it to the full."***

There is no ambiguity in Jesus' statement. He emphatically describes the enemy of all saints as a thief; one who attempts to deprive someone of their possessions by unlawfully taking them, either by force or trickery. He says the thief comes after believers only to commit three distinct crimes: steal, kill, and destroy. The ten commandments of God, given to Moses, list the commandments of God that every believer should abide by. "The Thief," as Jesus describes Satan, and as I introduced him in an earlier chapter as "a parasite in paradise," and he violates three of these commandments in his attempt to steal, kill, and destroy livelihood of believers.

First, Satan comes to steal because the commandments tell us not to steal. He comes to kill because the commandments say that we shall not kill. Finally, he comes to destroy because the commandment says that we shall not destroy others by coveting their belongings. The commandments advise us not to destroy a person's life by committing adultery. We shall not destroy our relationship with God by serving other gods. We shall not destroy our worship before God by forsaking the Sabbath day. Yet, the thief constantly devises schemes to cause violations in every one of these commandments. These acts of the thief are in dirtect contradiction to the word of God for His people. Then, Jesus goes on to describe to the believer as having a completely opposite nature compared to that of Satan. He says, "But, I come that you might have life and have it more abundantly."

This scripture let us know, without a shadow of a doubt, that God does not intend to destroy those who believe in Him. What God intends for the believer is for the believer to live a life full of peace, joy, and happiness. That is what abundant life is. It a life filled with meaning and purpose.

The "good news" is that the plans of God are designed to make his people's lives happy. Elihu tried to explain to his contemporaries that God is not their enemy. In his attempt to reveal to them the true nature of God, Elihu had only the understanding of Old Testament scripture, and his own personal relationship, in which to state his case.

We are fortunate to have the entire bible as our basis for an apologetic platform to defend the nature of God and, yet, some still unjustly blame God for their troubles. The 38th and 39th chapters of the book of Job warn us against taking the approach that we have the authority to question the sovereignty of God. In the 38th chapter, God asks Job hard questions that no man can answer.

It was like walking into a high school English class, and hearing the teacher say, "Today we are going to have a pop-quiz." You know that you are not prepared. You know that it is too late for you to quickly skim through the lesson, and possibly gleam some information that may help you. At this moment, your knees are weak, your throat becomes as dry as desert sand in July, and your brain simply locks up. You are in a desperate state of panic and confusion.

I can imagine that Job must have felt some similar emotions except that this is God almighty speaking in an audible voice, while calling you to the principal's office. God is giving Job an audible "pop-quiz" without the possibility of any worthy preparation. No textbook, not even the Holy Bible, could have prepared Job to answer these hard questions posed by God. Even the greatest scholars of today could not answer any of these hard questions. Study materials written by man can only answer what man already knows but God only reveals the deep secrets to man as He see fit to reveal them.

The questions asked of Job were what I refer to as "hard questions" because man has searched for hundreds of years, and is still light years away from being able to present a justifiable answer to the first question.

Then the Lord spoke to Job out of the storm. He said:

[2]"Who is this that obscures my plans with words without knowledge? 3 Brace yourself like a man; I will question you, and you shall answer me.

[4]"Where were you when I laid the earth's foundation? Tell me, if you understand.[5]Who marked off its dimensions? Surely you know! Who stretched a measuring line across it? [6]On what were its footings set, or who laid its cornerstone.

Job 38:1-6 (NIV)

Verse four sets the tone for all other hard questions asked of Job. Job was, unsuccessful in answering any of God's questions because they required wisdom that can only come from God.

In all of man's existence, from the beginning until now, many questions about this world we reside in are beyond our comprehension. God simply teaches us, through Job's ignorance, that we are no match to His wisdom and knowledge. If a thousand pages of this book could be written, it would not do justice in explaining all of the "hard questions" directed at Job in his dialog with God. In the final analysis of these two chapters, it is obvious that God knew that Job was in no position to question His actions. Man is limited in his knowledge. Therefore, we must learn to stay in our own lane, and let God be God. I am not implying that we should not question God in a general sense of questions to gain knowledge. I am stating that it is not wise for humans to question God's authority and wisdom.

I hope that, by reading this book, some mindsets will be changed or at the least that it will stir up some questions about our opinions of the nature of God, and His relationship with us as His creation - a creation made in His image, after His likeness, and in whom God has great hope. Trust and believe in the word of God, which was written for our benefit. Enjoy a life of joy in a personal relationship with Jesus. Rely on the word of God, and do not lean on your own limited understanding. In all your ways, acknowledge God as your source for life.

Chapter Eight
The Restoration of Job

The extraordinary storyline of the book of Job is that God is a merciful God who restores all that the enemy has stolen from His people. We must learn the art of trusting in the Lord, regardless of the circumstances. The beginning is seldom the same as the way things will end when we place our trust in God. David said in the Twenty-third Psalm, "He restores my soul." God have always been a restorer of His people. The Israelites were restored many times after taking up habitation with other gods, and forsaking the true God. Yet, God is merciful and just. He will not allow His word to return unto Him void of what He sent it out to do. God is a restorer! Salvation is the restoration of our souls.

In the New Testament writings, we find the story of the arrest and betrayal of Jesus. One of His disciples, Peter, had said that he would physically fight for Jesus. Peter was told that, not only would he not fight, but that he would betray his Lord three times before the rooster crowed.

Unfortunately for Peter, this prophecy came to pass and it caused great stress in Peter's life. But, God is a restorer!

After Jesus' resurrection, we read of the conversation between the Lord and Peter on the shore of Tiberias; Jesus asked Peter, "Do you love me more than these (other disciples)?"

Peter replied, "Yes, Lord, you know I love you."

Jesus said, "Feed my Lambs."

It may not seem to have much significance on face value but, in the course of what Peter went on to do in Jesus name, and with what is written in the books of first and second Peter, we see that Jesus left Peter with an awesome responsibility. Why would the Lord trust the leadership and world evangelism ministry to a man who had turned his back on him three days ago? The amazing lesson that Peter learned is that God is a restorer of those who trust Him.

In the 42nd chapter of the book of Job, we find a broken and contrite man who finally has come to the understanding of who God really is. He thought that he knew God. His love was certainly true for who he thought God was. However, God cannot be understood in simple terms, or in a single circumstance. God is a spirit and those who come to understand Him can only do so if they learn to worship Him in spirit and in truth. In other words, without spiritual discernments of God, and faith in Him, we cannot truly comprehend the fullness of God.

Job recognizes the omniscient and omnipotent power of God and that He is able to do any and all things; that His purpose is beyond any attempts to stop it. This is the beginning of a spiritual understanding of who God is in the supernatural.

Then Job replied to the Lord:

*2"I know that you can do all things; no purpose
of yours can be thwarted.*

*3You asked, 'Who is this that obscures my plans
without knowledge? Surely I spoke of things I
did not understand things too wonderful for me
to know4"You said, 'Listen now, and I will
speak; I will question you, and you shall
answer me.5My ears had heard of you but now*

my eyes have seen you.[6]Therefore I despise myself and repent in dust and ashes."

Job 42:1-6 (NIV)

The beginning of wisdom is to realize that God is more than an object of worship like other gods but, rather, He is the God of all creation.

Job declares his ignorance in speaking about the plans of God without the full spiritual knowledge of God's plans.

"My ears had heard of you, but now my eyes have seen you." What Job surmised is that just hearing about God alone does not give us enough understanding. But, he says, "Now my eyes have seen you." This means that Job's spiritual eyes have been opened to reveal just who God is! I explained this concept in an earlier chapter of this book, when talking about how the prophet's servant's eyes were opened so that he saw into the supernatural. One minute we are seeing things just as anyone sees them but, then, when our eyes are opened up into the supernatural realm, we see something totally different. The prophet's servant saw legions of angels on chariots of fire awaiting orders from the most high to do battle to save the prophet from the Assyrian army. The prophet said those who are for us are more than those that is against us. But, the servant only saw what his natural eyes could reveal, which is limited.

Job's eyes were opened to greater knowledge and wisdom because he acquired a greater personal relationship with his creator, and gained a greater level of trust in Him.

There are things of God that are only reveled to us individually when it is in God's timing and purpose. We may yearn for it earlier, or hope for it sooner, but our timing does not always line up with God's timeline and purpose for our lives. The key is to wait on the Lord, and do not become dependent upon our limited understanding. While we are waiting for God to give us clear sight, we should continue to trust and believe in Him.

For now we see only a reflection as in a mirror; then we shall see face to face. Now I know in part; then I shall know fully, even as I am fully known.

I Corinthians 13:12(NIV)

Notice that, even during the hardships endured by Job, God did not begin to peak until it was the right time. Once God started speaking to Job, understanding began to unveil itself. It was like a glass that was crystal clear in Job's sight as he came to the full knowledge of God. Job finally came to the realization that all of mankind was not to be compared with God. He also realized that the awesome power of God is beyond our understanding so we should not attempt to question what we cannot comprehend. If we continually acknowledge Him, He will direct our paths.

Now, having seen and obtained a greater understanding of God, Job realizes that he is not even worthy of further discussion. So, he wanted to do what people of his day did when they were ashamed or in mourning. *Job said, "Therefore I despise myself, and repent in dust and ashes."*

This revelation of God in the eyes of Job is so devastating that he can't bear it without humbling himself before the presence of God.

The good news is God is a restorer! God restored all that Job had lost, and also added to his wealth because Job passed the trials and test. Bildad, Eliphaz, and Zophar were the three friends of Job who came bearing bad news and criticism during his pain and suffering. Their words of scorn and ridicule toward Job and God caused them to receive the rebuke of God.

There still remained one final test for Job before he could be totally restored and that was the difficult task of praying for the very men who wrongfully accused him of sin.

Job 42:10"*And the Lord turned the captivity of Job, when he prayed for his friends: also the Lord gave Job twice as much as he had before.*

One area of our modern Christian walk that we struggle with is the Christ like attribute of loving and forgiving those who despitefully use us. It seems to be a human defense mechanism to defend ourselves in a self preservation attitude when we are harmed or wronged, especially when it was by someone we thought loved us. The three friends of Job had cruelly attacked his faithfulness, and the sovereignty of God, to a point of anger and distrust. So, the final hidden attribute of God, that we seldom give Him credit for, is His undying love for us. How he is faithful, slow to anger, and full of grace.

7 After the LORD had said these things to Job,
he said to Eliphaz the Temanite, "I am angry
with you and your two friends, because you
have not spoken the truth about me, as my
servant Job has. 8 So now take seven bulls and
seven rams and go to my servant Job and
sacrifice a burnt offering for yourselves. My
servant Job will pray for you and I will accept
his prayer and not deal with you according to
your folly. You have not spoken the truth about
me, as my servant Job has." 9 So Eliphaz the
Temanite, Bildad the Shuhite and Zophar the
Naamathite did what the LORD told them; and
the LORD accepted Job's prayer.

Job 42:7-9 (NIV)

It was God's grace that spoke to Job of the need to not only forgive his friends, but also to pray for them.

Job had to lay aside his own feelings of hurt in order to help his friends, who found themselves on the wrong side of the mercies of God. Jesus said that an act of human grace toward our enemies would be like heaping hot coals of ash upon their heads. As difficult as it is, we must learn to forgive, and pray for our enemies.

Blessing those who have despitefully used us is the ultimate Christian sacrifice of our flesh but it sets us apart from the worldly nature of man.

Job's latter days were better than his former years. Job suffered for a while but his suffering became rejoicing in the end. God is a restorer! Don't blame Him for your troubles because He has prepared everything necessary for our good, from the beginning of time. We must gain a stronger relationship with him so that we will have a relationship with Him built on trust, along with the knowledge that He will never leave us, nor forsake us. By His grace, we will end better than we began as it is His will for our lives.

Job lived to be a ripe old age, and was blessed all the days of his life because he trusted the Lord during and through his troubles. Through his trials and tribulations, Job discovered the truth that all of us would like to like to understand without the test. Job learned the "Gospel According to Elihu." That God does not bring about destruction on His people. That God is a loving God. God speaks continually whether we hear Him or not. God operates in grace and, without faith, it is impossible to please Him because they who come to God must first believe that He is! That He rewards those who seek Him with their whole hearts.

Relying on God with our sincere hearts, minds, and souls will give us the confidence to continue to press on each and every day.

“Maranatha.”

Works Cited

The Bible. Authorized King James Version, published as the Liberty Annotated Study Bible and the Annotated Study Bible, (King James Version), copyright 1988 by Liberty University.

The Holy Bible, New International Version. Copyright 1973, 1978, 1984 by International Bible Society.

NIV Witness Edition, Copyright 1986. All rights reserved, Published by Zondervan, Grand Rapids, Michigan 49530, U.S.A.

CPSIA information can be obtained
at www.ICGtesting.com
Printed in the USA
LVHW051450071222
734629LV00029B/1243

9 781958 877098